# THE

# DISC

# ADVANTAGE

C/C

## AN INTRODUCTORY GUIDE TO
## **LEVERAGING DISC ASSESSMENTS**
## FOR TEAM COHESION AND EFFECTIVENESS

chancellorcollective.com | 224-300-4925 | leadership@chancellorcollective.com

# Table of Contents

# Introduction

## Overview of DISC Assessments

### Definition and Brief History

DISC assessments are psychological tools developed to understand an individual's behavior, communication style, and temperament. The theory behind DISC is based on the work of psychologist William Moulton Marston in the 1920s, who identified four primary emotions and associated behavioral responses. DISC stands for:

| | | |
|---|---|---|
| **Dominance** | **D** | Direct, decisive, high ego strength, problem-solver |
| **Influence** | **I** | Outgoing, enthusiastic, optimistic, high-spirited, lively |
| **Steadiness** | **S** | Gentle, accommodating, soft-hearted, and loyal |
| **Conscientiousness** | **C** | Private, analytical, logical, and systematic |

**Purpose and Benefits of DISC in Organizational Settings**
DISC assessments are used in organizational settings to promote better teamwork, communication, and workplace productivity. They help managers and team leaders understand how team members prefer to work, and guide the development of more effective interactions within the team. The benefits of using DISC include:

 Improved self-awareness and understanding of personal behavior

 Enhanced understanding of how team members' behaviors interlock and where friction might occur

 Streamlined communication by appreciating the preferred styles of others

 Facilitated conflict resolution through a deeper understanding of underlying causes

 Optimized team performance by aligning tasks with natural behavioral strengths

**Importance of Team Cohesion and Effectiveness**

**Link Between Team Dynamics and Organizational Success**
Effective team dynamics are crucial for organizational success. Teams that work well together exhibit high levels of collaboration, communication, and mutual support, which in turn enhance productivity and job satisfaction. Strong team cohesion also leads to more innovative solutions and agility in responding to challenges, which are key competitive advantages in today's fast-paced business environments.

**Role of Personality Assessments in Understanding Team Dynamics**
Personality assessments, like DISC, play a significant role in understanding and shaping team dynamics. They provide a framework for deciphering complex human behaviors and can help predict how individuals are likely to interact with each other. Using DISC, leaders can:

 Identify and leverage diverse strengths within a team

 Develop strategies that accommodate various working styles

 Minimize conflicts and misunderstandings by acknowledging different needs and expectations

These insights allow leaders to foster an environment where all team members can thrive, contributing to overall team cohesion and effectiveness. This holistic approach not only bolsters individual and team performance but also aligns with strategic organizational goals.

Next, we'll delve into the specifics of each DISC profile in Section 1, detailing the characteristics, strengths, and potential areas for growth associated with Dominance, Influence, Steadiness, and Conscientiousness. This will provide a solid foundation for applying DISC principles effectively within teams.

As a certified DISC trainer and consultant, I bring a wealth of knowledge and practical experience to help organizations understand and apply DISC assessments effectively. My services include customized workshops and personalized coaching sessions that are designed to enhance team dynamics and improve overall workplace communication. **Contact me today to start your journey towards a more effective and harmonious team environment.**

# Section 1:

## Understanding DISC Profiles

### Explanation of the DISC Model

The DISC model categorizes four primary behavioral traits — Dominance, Influence, Steadiness, and Conscientiousness — each with distinct characteristics and tendencies. Understanding these traits allows teams to harness the diversity of behaviors to optimize their collaboration and productivity.

## Dominance (D):
## Characteristics, Strengths, and Potential Areas for Growth

### Characteristics:
Individuals with a high Dominance score are assertive, competitive, and decisive. They prefer to lead and are motivated by results and winning.

### Strengths:
Their ability to handle pressure and challenges head-on makes them excellent leaders in high-stakes environments. They are often very effective at cutting through red tape and making tough decisions.

### Potential Areas for Growth:
Their assertive nature can sometimes come off as aggressive or overly ambitious. Learning to temper their intensity and listen more can help them be more approachable and cooperative.

## Influence (I):
## Characteristics, Strengths, and Potential Areas for Growth

### Characteristics:
Those who score high in Influence are enthusiastic, optimistic, and persuasive. They are sociable and prefer collaborating and interacting with others.

### Strengths:
Their ability to inspire and motivate others makes them natural leaders, particularly in teams needing a morale boost or in roles that require rallying a group to achieve a common goal.

### Potential Areas for Growth:
They may struggle with over-talking and may overlook details. Developing more focus and learning to be more analytical can enhance their effectiveness.

 224-300-4925

leadership@chancellorcollective.com

### Steadiness (S):
### Characteristics, Strengths, and Potential Areas for Growth

**Characteristics:**
Steadiness is marked by calmness, patience, and loyalty. Individuals high in this trait are team players who value consistency and stability.

**Strengths:**
Their dependable nature makes them the backbone of many teams, providing the necessary support and consistency required for long-term success.

**Potential Areas for Growth:**
They may resist change and may not communicate dissatisfaction directly. Encouraging flexibility and open communication can help them become more adaptable and vocal.

### Conscientiousness (C):
### Characteristics, Strengths, and Potential Areas for Growth

**Characteristics:**
High scores in Conscientiousness indicate a preference for structure, precision, and detail. These individuals are analytical and cautious.

**Strengths:**
Their ability to maintain high standards and work within established systems makes them invaluable in roles that require accuracy and a methodical approach.

**Potential Areas for Growth:**
Their cautious nature can lead to indecision or a reluctance to take risks. Building confidence in decision-making and embracing some level of risk can aid in their professional growth.

224-300-4925

leadership@chancellorcollective.com

# Assessing DISC Profiles

**The Process of Conducting a DISC Assessment** Conducting a DISC assessment typically involves the following steps:

**Selection of a Suitable Assessment Tool:**
Choose a validated DISC assessment tool that meets the needs of the organization.

**Distribution and Completion:**
Distribute the assessment to team members and provide instructions for completing it. The assessment usually consists of a series of questions that respondents answer based on how they view themselves.

**Data Analysis:**
After completion, the tool analyzes the responses to categorize each participant into one of the DISC profiles.

**Interpreting Assessment Results** Interpreting the results of a DISC assessment involves:

**Reviewing Individual Profiles:**
Understand each team member's primary and secondary traits, focusing on their strengths and areas for growth.

**Contextualizing Within Team Dynamics:**
Analyze how different profiles interact with each other, identifying potential synergies and points of friction.

**Application to Workplace Scenarios:**
Tailor strategies for communication, conflict resolution, and task allocation based on the diverse behavioral styles present in the team.

By thoroughly understanding and applying the insights from DISC profiles, organizations can significantly enhance team effectiveness and create a more harmonious and productive work environment.

Enhance your team's communication and efficiency with tailored DISC workshops and training sessions. As a certified DISC trainer, I am dedicated to optimizing your team's performance by aligning their strengths with organizational goals. **Reach out now to see how your team can benefit from customized DISC training.**

# Section 2:

## Applying DISC in Teams

**Enhancing Team Communication**

**Strategies for Effective Communication Based on DISC Profiles** Effective communication in a team setting can be significantly enhanced by understanding and adapting to the diverse DISC profiles within the team. Here are tailored communication strategies for each DISC profile:

 **Dominance** **D**
Be clear, specific, and to the point. They prefer direct communication that does not waste time and focuses on results and solutions.

 **Influence** **I**
Engage them with enthusiastic, optimistic communication. They appreciate friendly, positive interactions and respond well to encouragement and lively discussions.

 **Steadiness** **S**
Provide gentle, sincere, and non-confrontational communication. They value harmony and stability, so ensure they are given time to process information and respond.

 **Conscientiousness** **C**
Offer detailed, accurate, and analytical communication. They respect data-driven and well-organized information, avoiding overly emotional or ambiguous language.

**Case Studies: Success Stories of Improved Communication**

 **Tech Startup:**
A tech startup utilized DISC assessments to tailor project updates and meeting styles, resulting in a 30% decrease in meeting times and a significant increase in measurable productivity.

 **Healthcare Team:**
A hospital department applied DISC principles to improve nurse-to-nurse handoffs, which enhanced patient care continuity and reduced errors due to miscommunication.

Leveraging my expertise as a certified DISC consultant, I specialize in facilitating conflict resolution strategies that are tailored to the unique behavioral styles of team members. My approach helps organizations turn potential conflicts into constructive dialogues, ensuring that teams not only understand but also appreciate their differences, leading to a more cohesive work environment. **Schedule Your Strategy Session Today!**

# Conflict Resolution

## Identifying Potential Conflicts Arising from Differing DISC Profiles

**D vs. S:** Dominance individuals' direct style might clash with Steadiness individuals' preference for calm and non-confrontational approaches.

**I vs. C:** Influence's informal and enthusiastic style may conflict with Conscientiousness's need for structure and detail.

## Mediation Strategies Tailored to DISC Dynamics

**Cross-profile understanding:**
Facilitate workshops that help team members understand the diverse communication styles and underlying motivations of different DISC profiles.

**Adaptive conflict management techniques:**
Train leaders to adapt their conflict resolution tactics based on the profiles of the individuals involved, such as using more structured problem-solving with C profiles and more open-ended, brainstorming approaches with I profiles.

# Role Allocation

Optimizing Team Performance Through Strategic Role Assignments Assign roles that naturally fit the behavioral strengths of each DISC profile, such as:

| | | |
|---|---|---|
| **Dominance** | **D** | Lead roles in crisis management or projects requiring decisive action. |
| **Influence** | **I** | Positions that require networking, motivating teams, or public speaking. |
| **Steadiness** | **S** | Supportive roles that require consistency and reliability, such as operations or customer service. |
| **Conscientiousness** | **C** | Roles that require attention to detail and precision, such as finance or compliance. |

 224-300-4925

 leadership@chancellorcollective.com

## Aligning DISC Profiles with Job Responsibilities

Implement a profiling step in the recruitment and team formation processes to ensure that individuals' natural strengths and job expectations align.

Use DISC insights for ongoing career development planning, helping employees grow into roles that suit their evolving profiles and aspirations.

By applying these strategies for enhancing communication, resolving conflicts, and allocating roles based on DISC profiles, teams can achieve greater cohesion, effectiveness, and overall performance. The understanding and intentional application of DISC principles empower organizations to harness the full potential of their workforce.

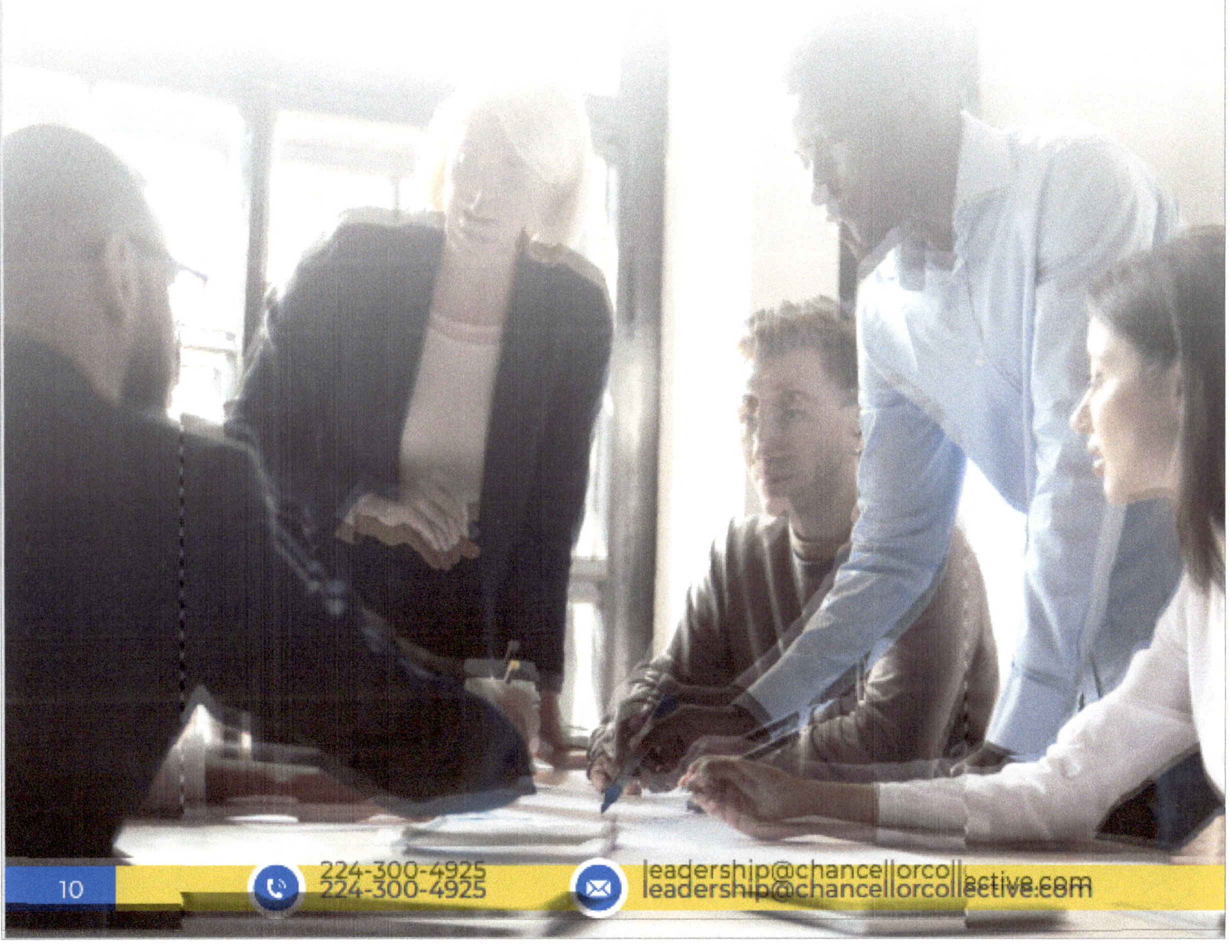

# Section 3:

## DISC for Leadership Development

**Leadership Styles and DISC**

**How Different DISC Profiles Influence Leadership Approaches** Each DISC profile lends itself to different leadership styles, and understanding these can enhance a leader's effectiveness by aligning their natural tendencies with the needs of their team:

 **Dominance (D):** Leaders with a high D profile are typically assertive, result-oriented, and authoritative. They excel in situations that require quick decision-making and crisis management. However, they need to be mindful of not overpowering their team members and should work on incorporating more collaborative approaches.

 **Influence (I):** These leaders are charismatic, persuasive, and excel in roles that require motivating others. They are effective at public speaking and rallying their teams toward a common vision. To balance their approach, they should focus on fostering substance over style and ensuring that their enthusiasm is backed by solid data and planning.

 **Steadiness (S):** Leaders who score high in Steadiness are dependable, supportive, and excel in creating a harmonious workplace. They are particularly effective in stable environments where they can focus on nurturing long-term relationships. Their challenge is to become more adaptable to change and more comfortable with ambiguity.

 **Conscientiousness (C):** Conscientious leaders are detail-oriented, logical, and excel in roles that require precision and meticulous planning. They thrive in environments where they can apply systems and processes. To enhance their leadership, they should work on being more flexible and faster in decision-making, especially in situations that do not afford the luxury of extensive data analysis.

**Adapting Leadership Style to Suit Diverse Team Profiles** Leaders can adapt their styles to better meet the needs of their diverse teams by:

**Using DISC insights:**
Understand the DISC profiles of team members and adjust communication and leadership tactics accordingly.

**Flexibility and empathy:**
Leaders should demonstrate flexibility in their approach and empathize with different team members' needs and preferences.

**Balanced teams:**
Construct teams with a balance of DISC profiles to cover various aspects of leadership and team dynamics effectively.

**Developing Emotionally Intelligent Leaders**
**The Role of DISC in Enhancing Emotional Intelligence** Emotional intelligence (EI) is critical for effective leadership, and DISC assessments can significantly enhance a leader's EI by providing deeper insights into their own emotional responses and those of their team members. DISC helps leaders:

**Self-awareness:**
Gain insights into their emotional strengths and weaknesses.

**Social awareness:**
Understand the emotional cues and needs of different DISC profiles.

## Techniques for Leaders to Adapt Based on Their and Their Team's DISC Profiles

**Self-regulation:**

Leaders can use their understanding of their own DISC profile to regulate their responses and adapt their behavior in ways that are more conducive to positive outcomes.

**Relationship management:**

By recognizing the DISC profiles of their team members, leaders can tailor their approach to managing relationships, ensuring more effective motivation, conflict resolution, and collaboration.

**Empathy exercises:**

Regular training and scenarios that allow leaders to practice empathy and understand different perspectives based on DISC profiles.

Incorporating DISC into leadership development not only equips leaders with the tools to understand and manage their teams better but also enhances their ability to lead with emotional intelligence. This leads to more cohesive, motivated, and effective teams that can navigate the complexities of the modern workplace with greater agility and success.

# Section 4:

## Measuring and Enhancing Effectiveness

### Monitoring Team Progress

**Tools and Methods for Assessing Team Performance Post-DISC Implementation** To effectively measure the impact of DISC assessments on team dynamics and performance, organizations can utilize the following tools and methods:

**Performance Metrics:**
Define specific, measurable metrics based on the goals set before DISC implementation, such as increased productivity, reduced conflict rates, or improved project completion times.

**360-Degree Feedback:**
Implement a comprehensive feedback system that allows team members to provide feedback on each other, including how well individuals are adapting to and integrating the insights gained from DISC assessments.

**Employee Engagement Surveys:**
Conduct regular surveys to gauge the level of engagement and satisfaction within the team, focusing on areas such as communication effectiveness and workplace harmony.

Incorporating DISC into leadership development not only equips leaders with the tools to understand and manage their teams better but also enhances their ability to lead with emotional intelligence. This leads to more cohesive, motivated, and effective teams that can navigate the complexities of the modern workplace with greater agility and success.

### Periodic Reassessment of DISC Profiles

Since individuals and teams evolve over time, periodic reassessment of DISC profiles is crucial:

**Scheduled Reassessments:**
Conduct DISC reassessments annually or biennially to track changes in team dynamics and individual profiles.

**Event-Triggered Reassessments:**
In addition to scheduled reassessments, consider re-evaluating DISC profiles after significant organizational changes, such as major projects, team restructuring, or leadership shifts.

**Continuous Improvement**

**Using Feedback to Refine Team Strategies** Feedback gathered from various sources, including performance reviews and DISC reassessments, should be utilized to refine team strategies continually. This process includes:

**Actionable Insights:**
Analyze feedback to identify actionable insights that can directly impact team management and development strategies.

**Strategy Adjustments:**
Based on feedback, adjust communication approaches, conflict resolution tactics, and role allocations to better suit the evolving dynamics of the team.

**Case Studies: Organizations That Successfully Implemented Ongoing DISC Training**

**Global Consulting Firm:**
This firm introduced DISC assessments during a period of high turnover and low morale. By integrating continuous DISC training and periodic reassessments into their development programs, they saw a 40% improvement in employee retention and a significant increase in client satisfaction scores.

**Healthcare Provider:**
A major healthcare provider implemented ongoing DISC training to improve interdepartmental collaboration. The training focused on understanding and respecting diverse communication styles, leading to a 30% reduction in internal conflicts and an enhancement in team collaboration across departments.

By monitoring team progress and implementing a cycle of continuous improvement based on DISC insights, organizations can create a more dynamic, responsive, and effective team environment. This not only optimizes individual and team performance but also aligns organizational strategies with actual team dynamics, fostering a culture of continuous learning and adaptation.

Through my ongoing support as a DISC consultant, I assist teams in integrating continuous improvement practices into their daily operations. By providing regular DISC reassessments and actionable feedback, I help teams remain agile and responsive to changing dynamics, thereby sustaining performance improvements over time. **Book a free call to learn more.**

# Conclusion

## Summary of Key Points

Throughout this guide, we have explored the foundational aspects and practical applications of DISC assessments in enhancing team cohesion and effectiveness. Key takeaways include:

### Understanding DISC Profiles:
Recognizing the unique characteristics, strengths, and growth areas of Dominance (D), Influence (I), Steadiness (S), and Conscientiousness (C) profiles is crucial for leveraging individual strengths and addressing potential weaknesses within teams.

### Applying DISC in Teams:
Effective communication strategies, conflict resolution, and role allocation based on DISC profiles can significantly improve team dynamics and productivity.

### Leadership Development:
DISC assessments provide valuable insights that help leaders adapt their styles to suit diverse team profiles, enhancing their emotional intelligence and leadership effectiveness.

### Measuring and Enhancing Effectiveness:
Ongoing monitoring and continuous improvement through DISC tools and feedback mechanisms are essential for sustaining high team performance and alignment with organizational goals.

## Encouraging a Culture of Continuous Learning and Adaptation

Adopting DISC assessments is not just about a one-time improvement in team functions but fostering a culture of continuous learning and adaptation. Organizations that embrace this approach benefit from:

### Enhanced Self-Awareness:
Regular DISC reassessments encourage individuals to remain aware of their evolving behavioral styles and how these changes impact their interactions and performance.

### Dynamic Team Adaptation:
Continuous learning about DISC profiles helps teams adapt to changes in their composition and environment, maintaining effectiveness regardless of external pressures.

### Proactive Conflict Management:
A deep understanding of DISC dynamics allows teams to anticipate and mitigate conflicts before they escalate, promoting a harmonious work environment.

## Final Thoughts on the Transformative Power of DISC Assessments in the Workplace

DISC assessments offer more than just an analytical tool; they provide a transformative framework for understanding and harnessing the diverse human elements within an organization. When integrated into regular training and development programs, DISC assessments empower individuals and teams to perform at their best, adapt to changes, and effectively contribute to their organization's success.

By committing to the principles outlined in this guide, leaders can unlock the full potential of their teams, fostering an environment where collaboration flourishes and productivity thrives. In the journey towards organizational excellence, DISC assessments serve as a compass, guiding teams through the complexities of human behaviors and interpersonal dynamics.

If you're looking to transform your team's dynamics and enhance leadership capabilities through DISC assessments, I can help. As a seasoned DISC consultant, I offer strategic advice and continuous support to integrate these powerful tools into your daily operations, helping you achieve and sustain high performance and team cohesion. **Let's connect to discuss how we can elevate your organizational success together. Schedule your free consultation today!**

# Appendices

## Appendix A: Further Reading on DISC and Team Management

To deepen your understanding of DISC assessments and their application in team management, consider the following resources:

 **The DISC Assessment:** Understanding Personality to Increase Team Performance" - by Robert A. Cooke

 **Positive Personality Profiles:** Discover Personality Insights to Understand Yourself and Others" - by Robert A. Rohm

224-300-4925

leadership@chancellorcollective.com

## Glossary

**Dominance (D):**
The trait characterized by assertiveness, decisiveness, and high ego strength.

**Influence (I):**
**The trait showing sociability, talkativeness, and emotional expressiveness.**

**Steadiness (S):**
**Represents calmness, patience, and loyalty.**

**Conscientiousness (C):**
**Denotes precision, analysis, and systematic approaches.**

**Emotional Intelligence:**
**The ability to understand, use, and manage one's own emotions positively to relieve stress, communicate effectively, empathize with others, overcome challenges, and defuse conflict.**

# References

For further research and verification of the information presented in this guide, refer to the following sources:

**Marston, W. M.** "Emotions of Normal People". London: Kegan Paul, Trench, Trubner & Co, Ltd. (1928): Provides foundational theories behind the DISC model.

**Robbins, Tony.** "DISC Training Workbook": Offers practical exercises and deeper insights into applying DISC assessments in various settings.

**"Journal of Business Psychology":** Frequently publishes research and case studies on the application of personality assessments, including DISC, in organizational settings.

These resources will provide both the theoretical background and practical insights needed to effectively implement and benefit from DISC assessments in enhancing organizational performance and leadership development.

 224-300-4925 |  leadership@chancellorcollective.com

**Scan this QR code to visit our
website and explore more!**

# Additional Information

# About Chancellor Collective

Welcome to Chancellor Collective, where leadership, inclusivity, and innovation intersect to create a thriving community. At Chancellor Collective, we believe in the power of transformative leadership and the profound impact it can have on individuals and organizations alike.

## Who We Are

Chancellor Collective is more than a consultancy; it's a movement dedicated to fostering effective leadership and promoting diversity, equity, and inclusion (DEI) in the workplace. Founded by a passionate leader with a wealth of experience in both the military and corporate sectors, our mission is to empower leaders and organizations to reach their full potential through strategic guidance, personalized coaching, and impactful training.

## Our Values

- **Integrity:** We operate with the highest level of integrity in all our interactions. Trust and honesty are the cornerstones of our relationships with clients and partners.
- **Empowerment:** We are committed to empowering individuals and teams by providing them with the tools and support they need to succeed. We believe in the potential of every person to lead and make a difference.
- **Authenticity:** We champion authenticity in all our endeavors, encouraging leaders to be true to themselves and their values. We believe that genuine leadership fosters trust, respect, and deeper connections within teams and organizations.
- **Inclusivity:** Diversity and inclusion are at the heart of what we do. We strive to create environments where everyone feels valued, respected, and able to contribute their unique perspectives.
- **Excellence:** We pursue excellence in all our endeavors. Our goal is to deliver outstanding results that exceed expectations and drive meaningful change.
- **Collaboration:** We believe in the power of collaboration. By working together and leveraging the strengths of diverse teams, we can achieve greater innovation and success.

## Our Services

At Chancellor Collective, we offer a comprehensive range of services designed to meet the unique needs of our clients:

- **Leadership Development:** Our leadership programs are tailored to help leaders at all levels enhance their skills, build resilience, and lead with confidence. From emerging leaders to seasoned executives, we provide the insights and strategies needed to excel.
- **DEI Training and Consulting:** We help organizations develop and implement effective DEI strategies that foster inclusive cultures and drive sustainable change. Our training sessions and workshops are designed to raise awareness, promote understanding, and inspire action.

- **Executive Coaching:** Our personalized coaching services are designed to support leaders in navigating challenges, achieving their goals, and unlocking their full potential. We provide one-on-one guidance and support to help leaders thrive.
- **Team Building:** We offer team-building workshops and activities that enhance collaboration, communication, and trust within teams. Our goal is to create cohesive, high-performing teams that can achieve extraordinary results.
- **DISC Consulting:** We offer comprehensive DISC assessments and consulting services to help individuals and teams understand their behavioral styles. By leveraging DISC insights, we enhance communication, collaboration, and overall team performance, enabling leaders to better understand themselves and their team members for more effective leadership.

## Our Approach

We take a holistic and personalized approach to leadership and DEI. By understanding the unique challenges and opportunities within each organization, we tailor our services to meet specific needs and drive impactful results. Our approach is rooted in real-world experience, best practices, and a deep commitment to creating positive change.

## Why Choose Chancellor Collective

Choosing Chancellor Collective means choosing a partner dedicated to your success. We bring a unique blend of military precision, corporate experience, and a passion for leadership and inclusivity to every engagement. Our clients benefit from our:

- **Expertise:** With years of experience and a deep understanding of leadership and DEI, we provide expert guidance and support.
- **Commitment:** We are committed to making a difference. Our work is driven by a genuine desire to empower individuals and transform organizations.
- **Results:** We focus on delivering measurable results that drive real change. Our success is measured by the success of our clients.

## Join Us on the Journey

We invite you to join us on the journey to better leadership, greater inclusivity, and lasting impact. Whether you're looking to develop your leadership skills, enhance your organization's DEI efforts, or build stronger teams, Chancellor Collective is here to support you every step of the way.

Together, we can create a brighter, more inclusive future. Welcome to Chancellor Collective.

# Overview of Our Services

### Training

Book an impactful lunch and learn session, based on John Maxwell's principles, designed to boost your leadership skills in a convenient and engaging format. Learn more below.

### Workshops

Dive deep into our half-day or full day workshops, offering practical tools and strategies to elevate your leadership effectiveness.

### Masterminds

Participate in our 6-10 week masterminds, where you'll collaborate with fellow leaders fostering sustained personal and professional growth. Keep scrolling to learn more.

## Training

**Unlock Your Leadership Potential - Schedule Your Session Today!**

Elevate your leadership skills with our dynamic lunch and learn sessions, tailored for groups of 5 to 500. Our expert-led trainings are designed to fit seamlessly into your schedule, providing actionable insights and strategies that you can apply immediately. Whether you're looking to enhance team collaboration, improve decision-making, or inspire your organization, our sessions based on John Maxwell's principles will empower you to lead with confidence and impact. Don't miss this opportunity to transform your leadership potential—*book your training session today and start making a difference!*

## Workshops

**Transform Your Leadership - Book Your Half or Whole Day Workshop!**

Elevate your organization's leadership effectiveness with our intensive half-day or full day workshops, perfect for groups of up to 60 people. These sessions are designed to provide your team with practical tools and strategies that can be implemented immediately to drive success. Through hands-on activities and deep discussions, we'll challenge your team's thinking and enhance their leadership capabilities. Don't miss this opportunity to transform your approach to leadership—*book your workshop now and start making a lasting impact!*

## Masterminds

**Cultivate Excellence - Book Your Leadership Mastermind Today!**

Take your leadership to the next level with our 6-10 week mastermind sessions, designed for groups of 10 to 40. Meet for an hour or two each week (virtually or in person) to collaborate with fellow leaders, exploring advanced strategies and concepts that foster sustained personal and professional growth. Our mastermind format encourages deep learning and practical application, ensuring you achieve meaningful, lasting results. Elevate your leadership journey—*contact us today to schedule your mastermind series and start cultivating excellence!*

\*Additional products and services offered are Digital Courses, Youth Programming, Books, and Awareness Apparel

# Overview of Our Services

## DEI Coaching

**Empower Your DEI Leaders—Contact Us Today**

Our DEI coaching services are designed to support ERG leaders, DEI councils, and business executives in creating inclusive workplaces. We provide personalized coaching to develop effective DEI strategies and foster a culture of belonging.

- ✔ **ERG Leaders**
- ✔ **DEI Councils**
- ✔ **Business Leaders and Executives**

## ERG Consulting

**Optimize Your ERGs—Schedule Your Consultation**

From comprehensive ERG management to launching and optimizing your ERGs, our consulting services offer tailored solutions to enhance the impact and effectiveness of your employee resource groups.

- ✔ **Comprehensive ERG Management** (High-Touch)
- ✔ **ERG Launch & Facilitation** (Mid-Touch)
- ✔ **ERG Growth & Optimization** (Mid-Touch)

## Inclusive Leadership Training

**Develop Inclusive Leaders—Enroll in Our Training Programs**

Our engaging inclusive leadership training focuses on key topics to enhance leadership skills and promote an inclusive culture. Choose from half-day or full-day live training packages, or opt for licensed training for ongoing development.

- ✔ **1/2 Day Training Live**
- ✔ **Whole Day Training Live**
- ✔ **Licensed Training**

## "Done-For-You" Customized Packages

**Streamline Your ERG Success—Explore Our Packages**

Whether you need to launch, optimize, or grow your ERGs, our done-for-you packages provide comprehensive solutions to ensure your ERGs are effective and aligned with your organizational goals.

- ✔ **Launch Your ERGs**
- ✔ **Optimize Your ERGs**
- ✔ **Grow Your ERGs**

## Custom Built Corporate Packages

**Tailored Solutions to Meet Your Unique Needs**

Our custom-built corporate packages are designed to address your specific organizational challenges and goals. Whether you need a bespoke leadership training program, DEI strategy, or comprehensive ERG management, we work closely with you to create a tailored solution that drives results.

- ✔ Personalized assessment and strategy development
- ✔ Custom training and coaching sessions
- ✔ Ongoing support and progress tracking

## Don't See What You're Looking For?

**Let Us Know and We'll Create a Solution for You**

If our listed services don't fully meet your needs, we're here to help. Contact us to discuss your specific requirements, and we'll work with you to develop a customized solution that fits your organization perfectly. Your success is our priority.

- ✔ Flexible and adaptable service options
- ✔ Collaborative approach to solution design
- ✔ Commitment to your unique organizational goals

# Thank You

First off, thank you from the bottom of my heart for taking the time to dive into "The DISC Advantage." Your commitment to bettering yourself and your team by engaging with this material means more than words can express. It's readers like you who inspire and drive the creation of resources like this, aiming to transform the workplace into a more effective and harmonious environment.

In a world that moves so fast, taking the time to read and apply the concepts in this guide is a testament to your dedication to growth and excellence. It's my sincere hope that the insights you've gained here will not only enhance your understanding of DISC assessments but also empower you and your team to reach new heights of success.

Whether you're looking to resolve conflicts more smoothly, communicate more effectively, or boost team cohesion, the journey you're embarking on with this knowledge is invaluable. I am thrilled to be a part of that journey and am eager to hear how you've implemented these strategies within your own teams.

Remember, the path to improvement is ongoing, and every small step you take is a leap towards greater achievements. Thank you once again for your trust and engagement. Let's continue to grow and learn together, pushing the boundaries of what our teams can accomplish.

With gratitude and best wishes for your continued success,

Clera

# What It's Like to Work With Me

What It's Like to Work With Me

Ciera always has a positive attitude and fosters both teamwork and proficiency in a climate of dignity and respect.

John Go.

I recommend Ciera to any organization willing to embrace change and win at the next level.

Brian D.

Great job presenting to our president and CEO. Your passion was contagious.

John Gi.

Ciera is engaging and smart and has unlimited potential.

Mike H.

Observing Ciera throughout the execution of her work made it abundantly clear that she is an exceptionally dedicated and caring leader.

Gary B.

Ciera clearly brings humble intelligence and passion to her work. She strives to make a meaningful impact and is always collaborative, polite, and supportive.

Jodi S.

It was a pleasure to work with Ciera and be part of her team. She is a great leader and good person. Her ability to maintain a positive and productive environment helped us to build and expand a strong Veteran's Network.

Ilya C.

Ciera's creativity, courage and enthusiasm were infectious. I can't thank her enough for her tireless efforts to listen, support and act with urgency to help people feel a strong sense of belonging.

Michael J.

Ciera is passionate about people, integrity, and work ethics. I had the pleasure to partner with her in varied capacities over several years. Ciera is professional, solid and always has a positive can-do attitude.

Audrey H.

I worked with Ciera on our Flex Network, and I can say that she passionate, always dedicated to work with, such a pleasure to work and always natural preacher, she always came prepared and looks after about everyone and make for was to make a dynamic She one great to at achieving every new goal. Her positivity communicated. Her positivity is contagious.

Suthar B.

Ciera's leadership in our department was something else. She went above and beyond to make sure our team felt supported and connected. Working with her was a real eye-opener to what a true leader should be someone who not only gets things done, but also looks out for everyone's well-being.

Amanda V.

Her leadership style was empowering, inclusive, and truly commendable. Ciera trusted the committee leaders and elevated contributions by showcasing them to senior leadership and other ERGs. Her global mindset, recognition of hard work, and commitment to impact, created an inclusive and motivating work environment.

Simon R.